# Insects

## The world according to bugs!

Houseflies find sugar with their feet, which are 10 million times more sensitive than human tongues.

Ticks can grow from the size of a grain of rice to the size of a marble.

Approximately 2000 silk worm cocoons are needed to produce one pound of silk.

While gathering food, a bee may fly up to 60 miles in one day.

Ants can lift and carry more than fifty times their own weight.

Wasps feeding on fermenting juice have been known to get drunk and pass out.

Honeybees make about 10 million trips to collect enough nectar for one pound of honey.

Night butterflies have ears on their wings so they can avoid bats.

Locusts can eat their own weight in food a day. Humans eat their own weight in about six months.

Honeybees have hair on their eyes.

**If you want to improve your perspective on life and clarify issues begin writing in a journal.**

_____
_____
_____
_____
_____
_____
_____
_____
_____
_____
_____
_____
_____
_____
_____
_____
_____
_____
_____
_____
_____
_____
_____
_____
_____
_____
_____
_____
_____

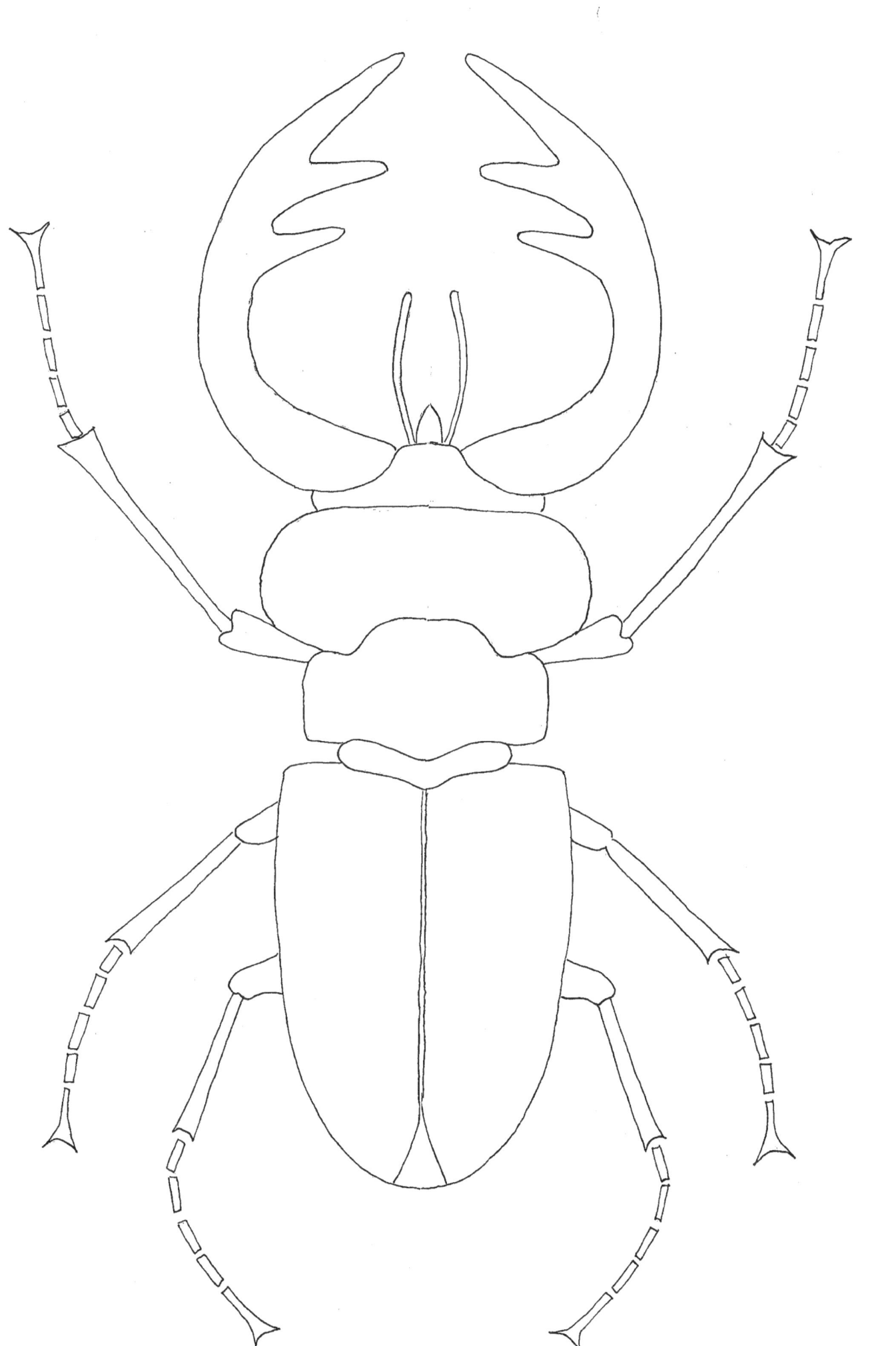

Journaling can help you process through failed relationships as well as recover from grief and loss.

_____
_____
_____
_____
_____
_____
_____
_____
_____
_____
_____
_____
_____
_____
_____
_____
_____
_____
_____
_____
_____
_____
_____
_____
_____
_____
_____
_____
_____
_____
_____
_____
_____

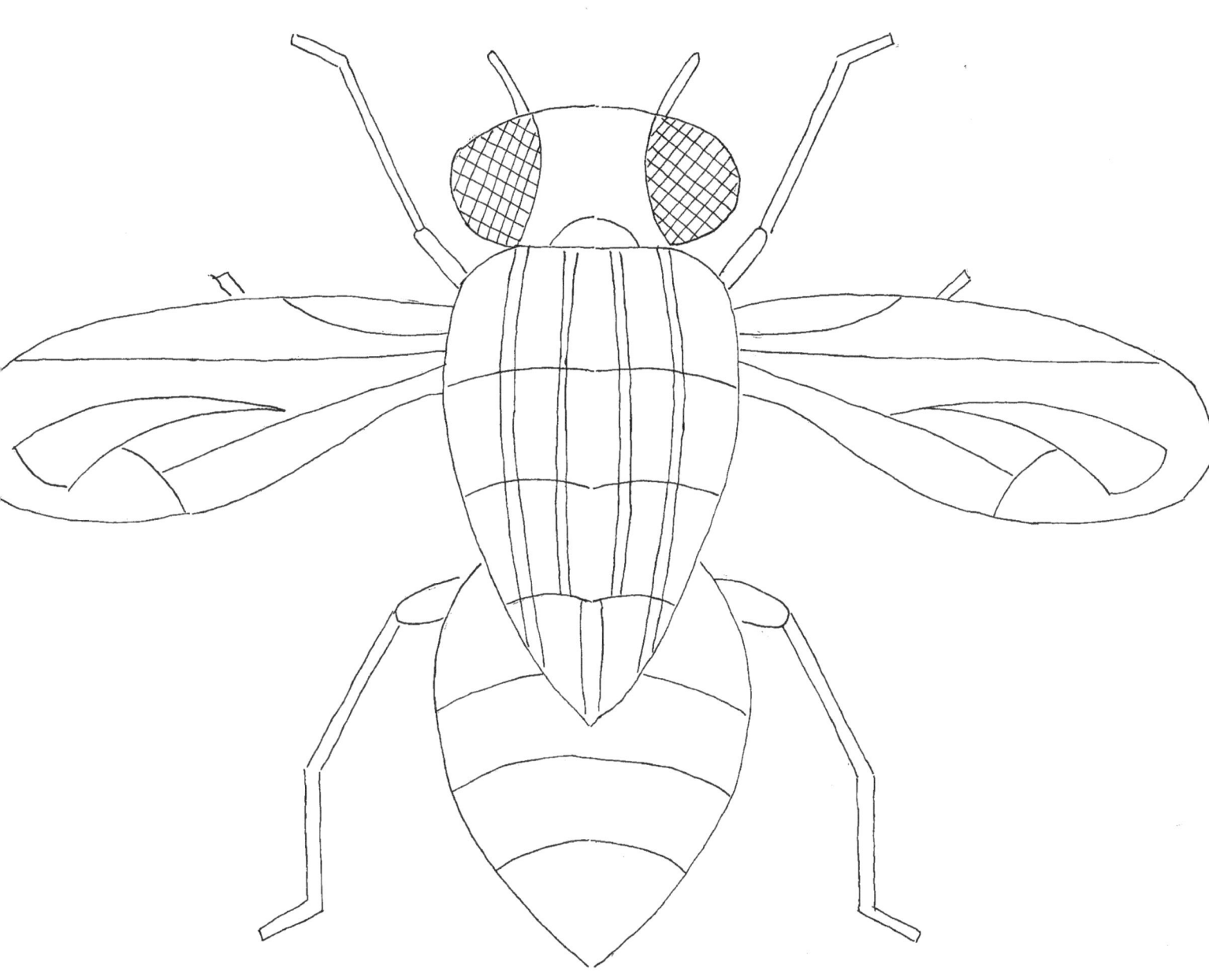

# Journaling can help you see opportunities that may not have been apparent to you at first glance.

_____

_____

_____

_____

_____

_____

_____

_____

_____

_____

_____

_____

_____

_____

_____

_____

_____

_____

_____

_____

_____

_____

_____

_____

_____

_____

_____

_____

_____

_____

_____

_____

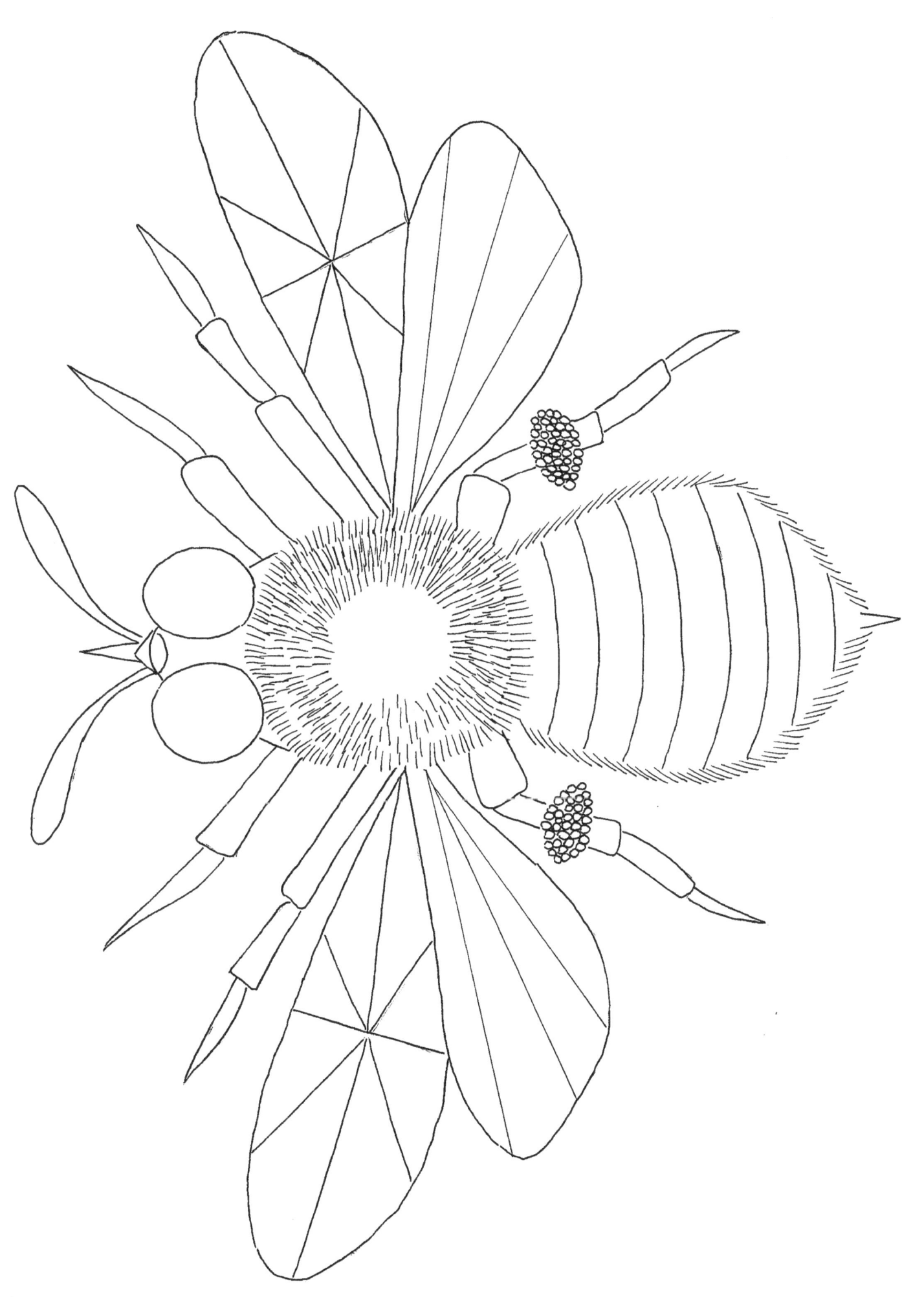

A transition journal is a record of any transition you are going through,
such as a job, becoming a parent, starting a business, or a new stage of life
you are entering.

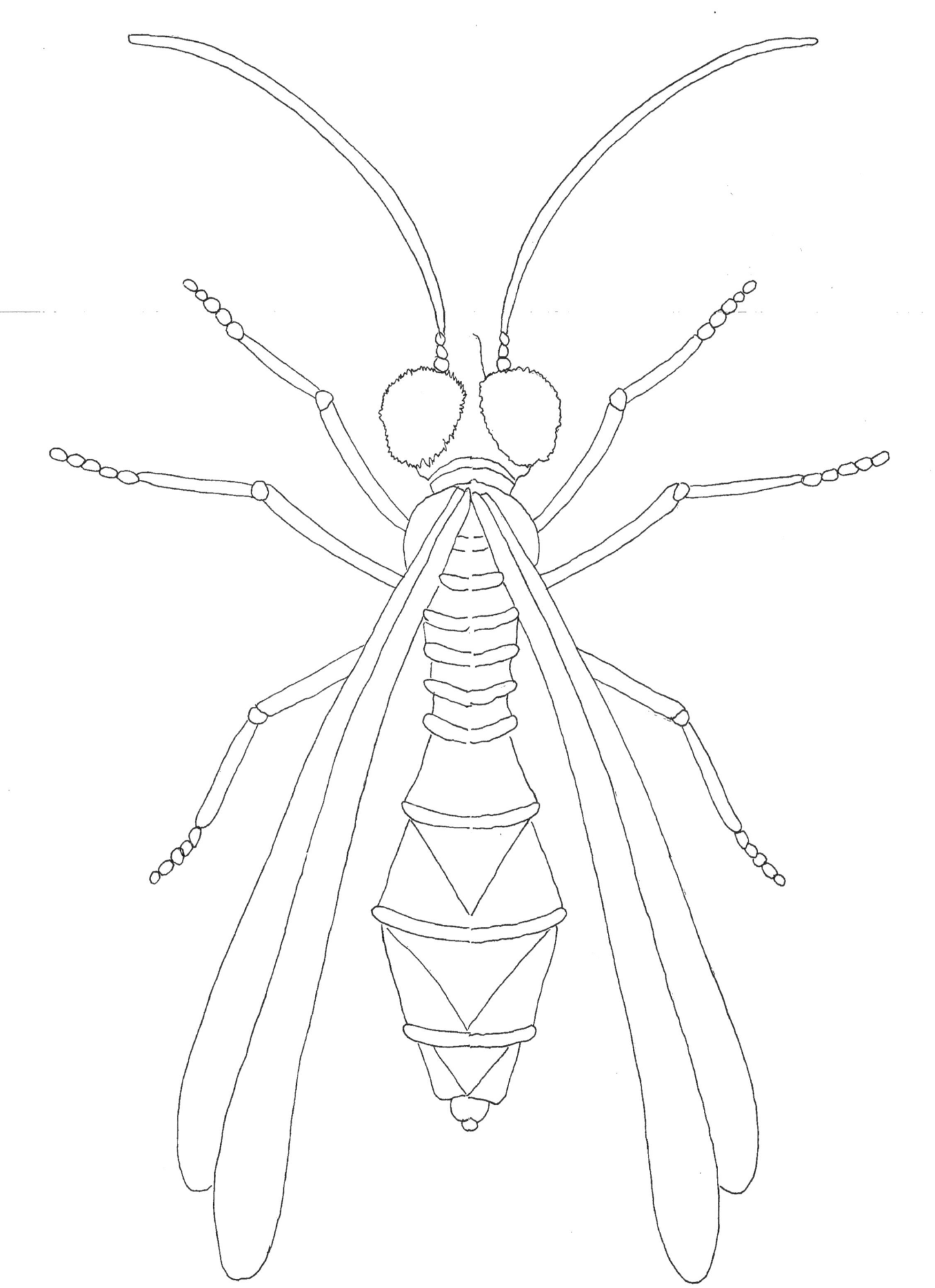

A child journal can include all the things that you feel are special, wonderful, lovable, and memorable about your kids or grandkids at different ages and stages of life.

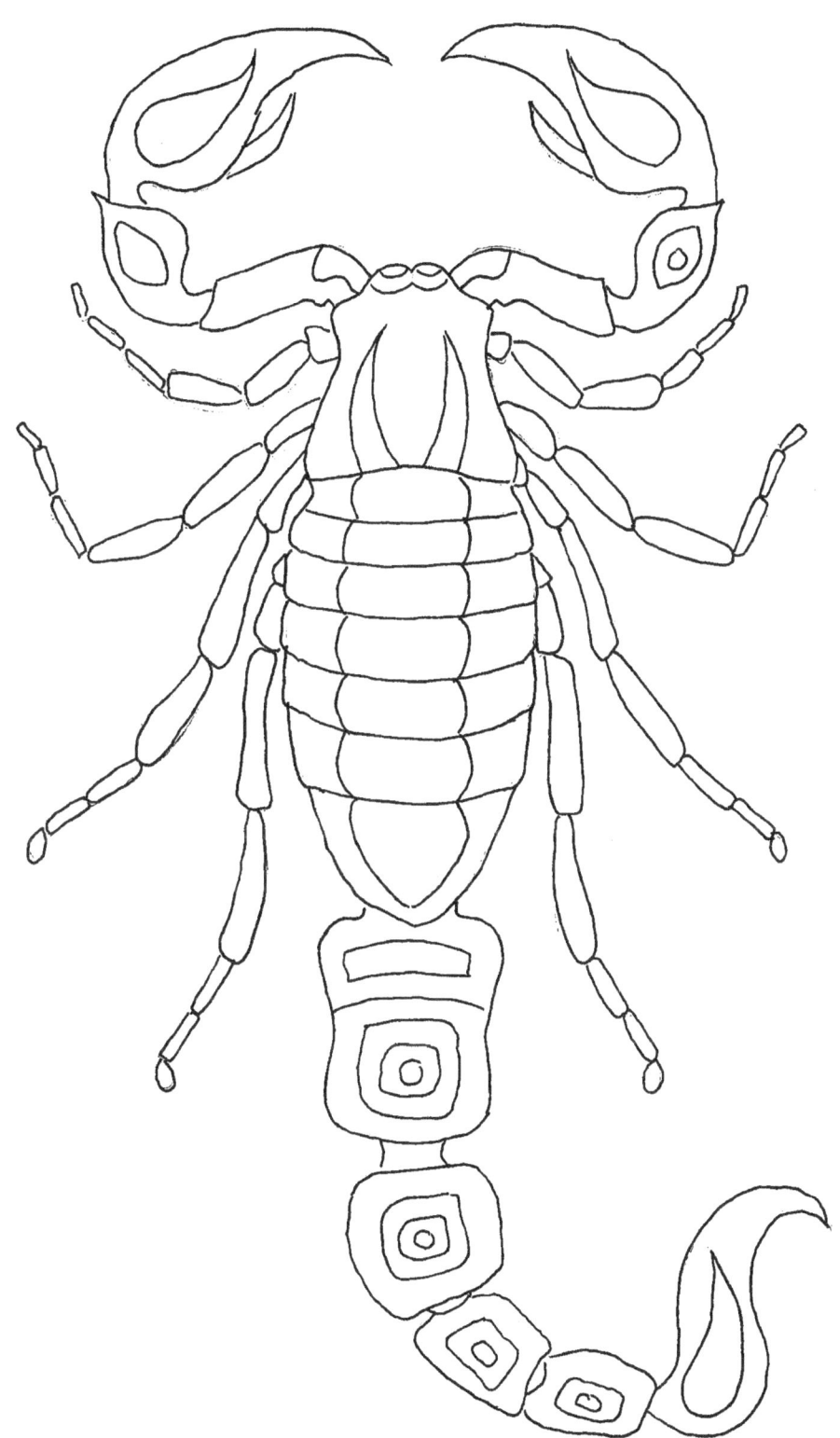

# Journaling is about reflection and solitude.

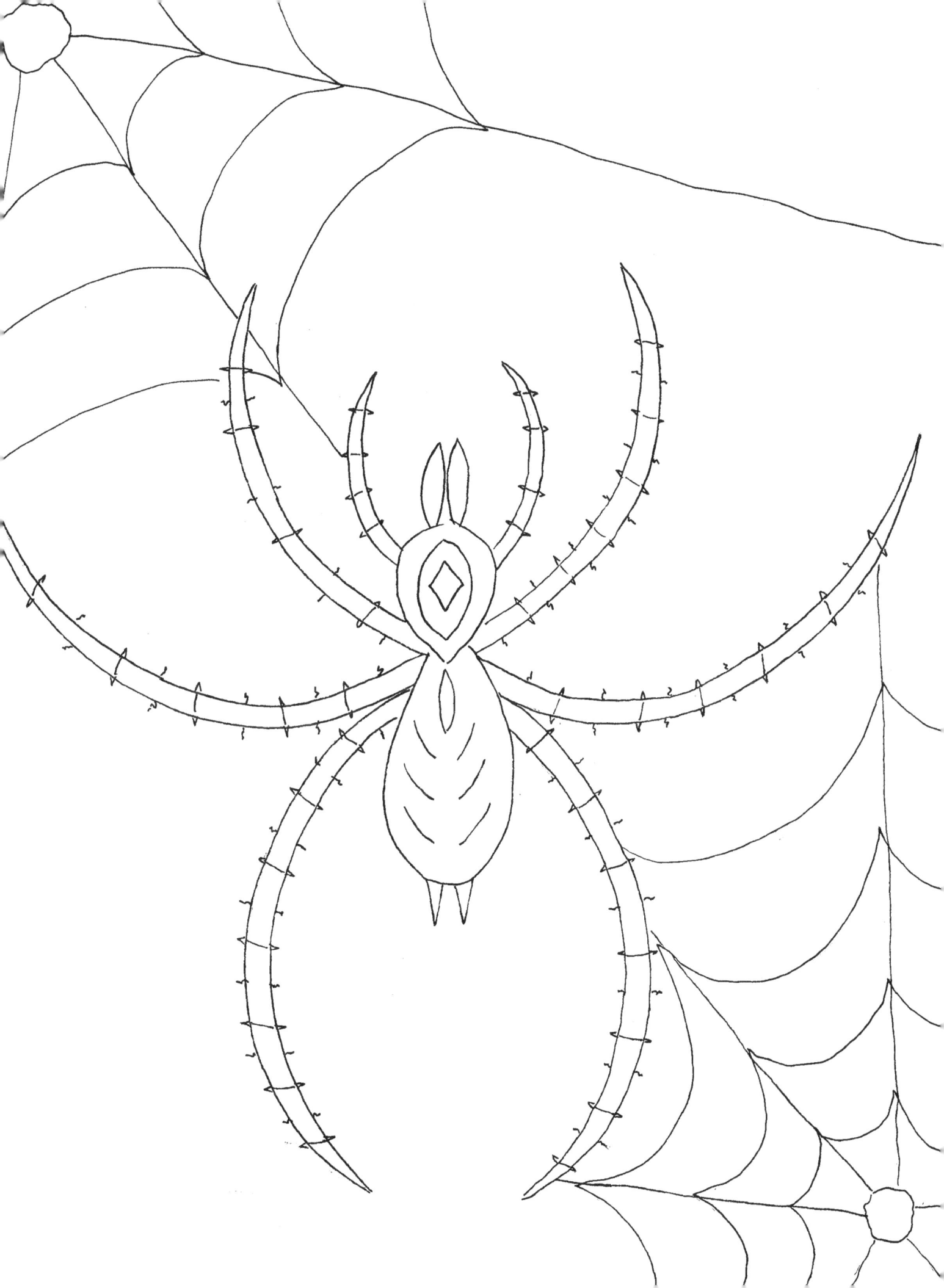

Journals are a great place to collect phrases, sayings, comments, quotes and notes from the world of life.

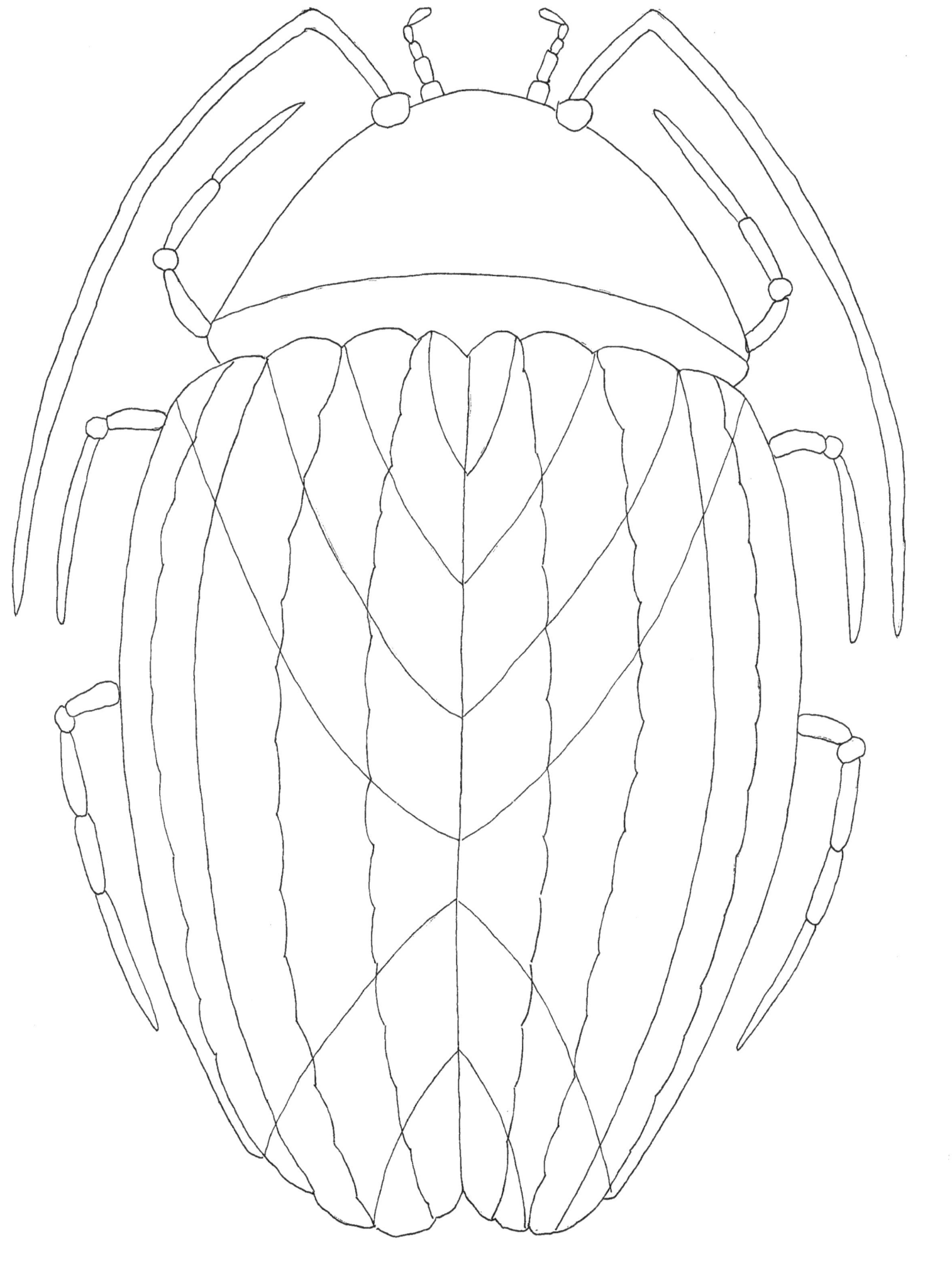

# Journaling helps with personal growth and development.

_____
_____
_____
_____
_____
_____
_____
_____
_____
_____
_____
_____
_____
_____
_____
_____
_____
_____
_____
_____
_____
_____
_____
_____
_____
_____
_____
_____
_____
_____
_____

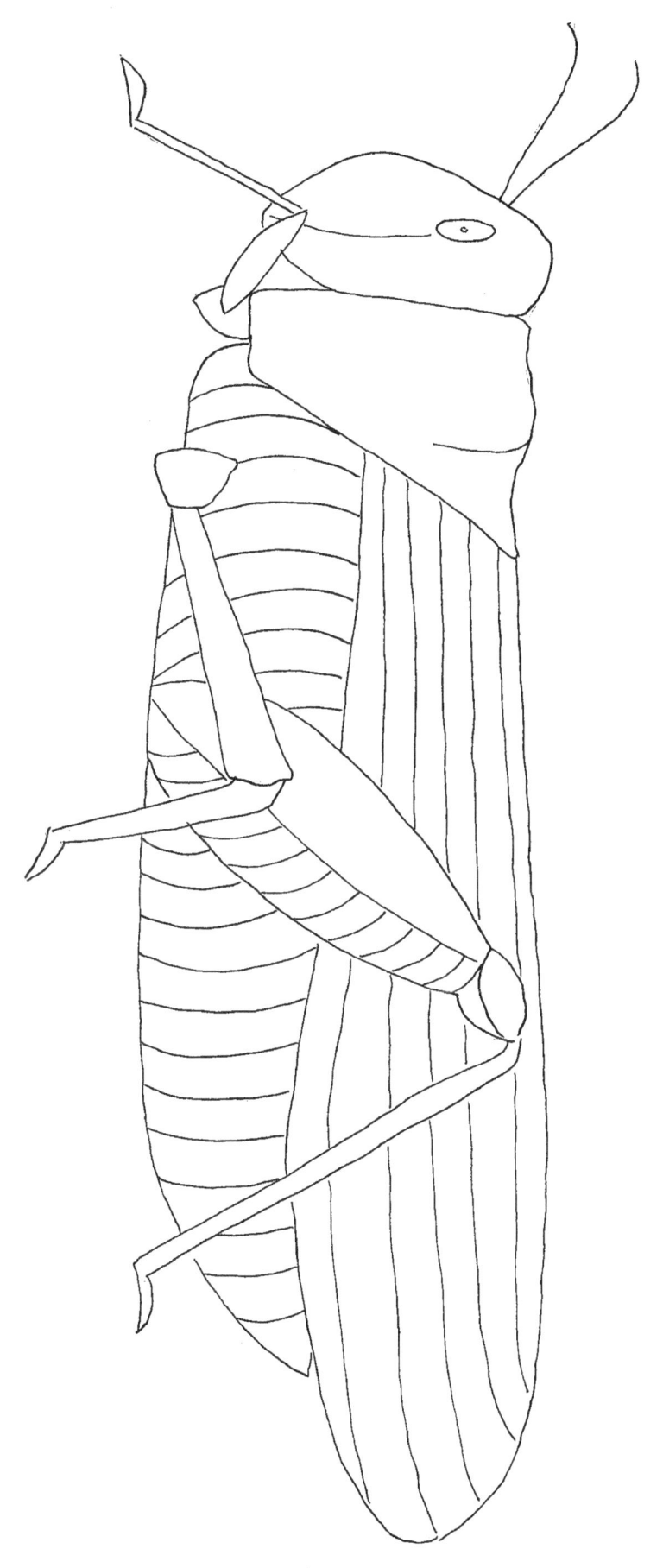

Journaling can be used for problem-solving and a stress reliever.

_____

_____

_____

_____

_____

_____

_____

_____

_____

_____

_____

_____

_____

_____

_____

_____

_____

_____

_____

_____

_____

_____

_____

_____

_____

_____

_____

_____

_____

_____

_____

_____

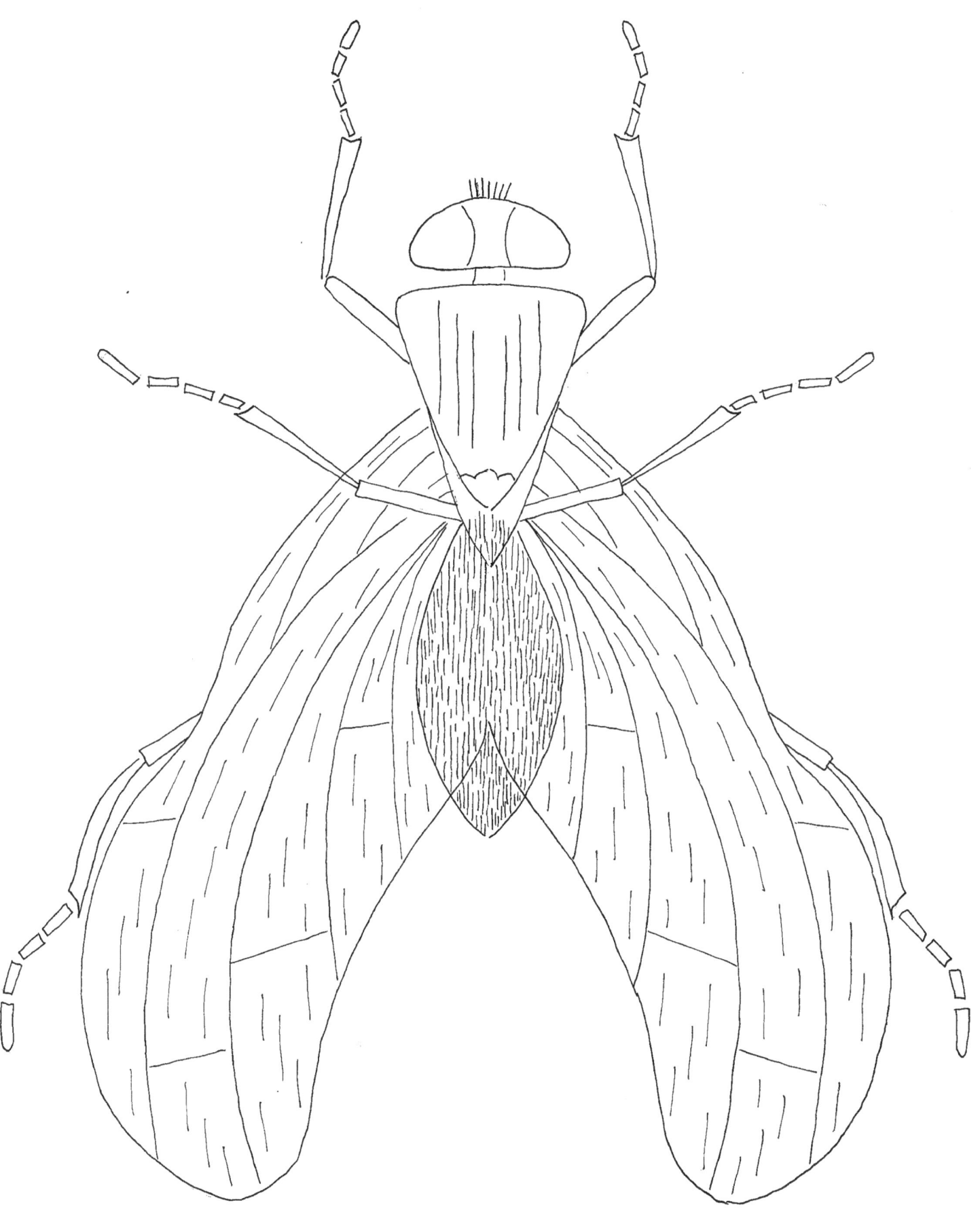

**Every person differs in what helps them to relax and feel contented. Coloring and writing go hand in hand!**

---

---

---

---

---

---

---

---

---

---

---

---

---

---

---

---

---

---

---

---

---

---

---

---

---

---

---

---

---

---

---

---

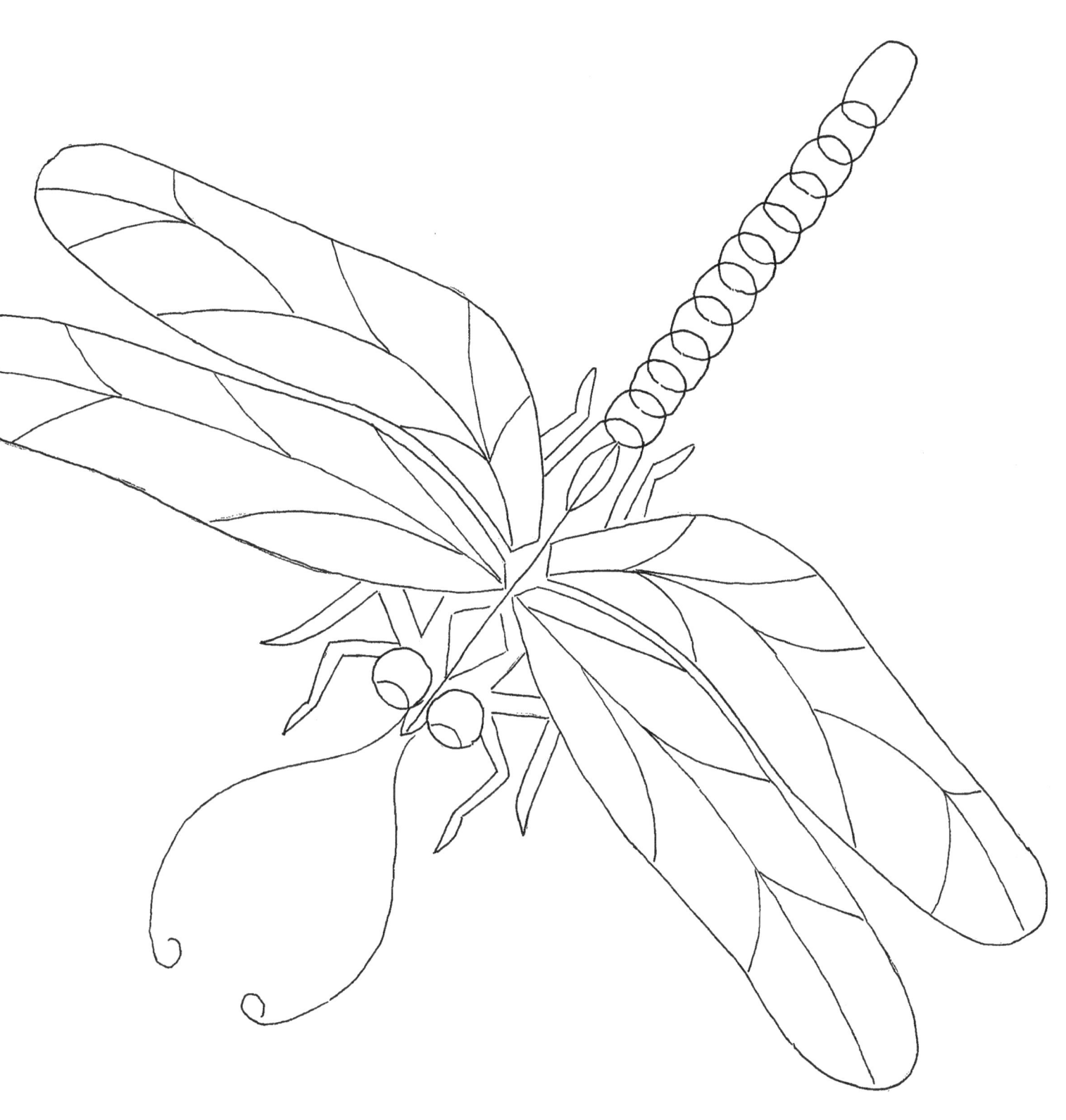

# Journaling can lead to increased self-esteem.

_____

_____

_____

_____

_____

_____

_____

_____

_____

_____

_____

_____

_____

_____

_____

_____

_____

_____

_____

_____

_____

_____

_____

_____

_____

_____

_____

_____

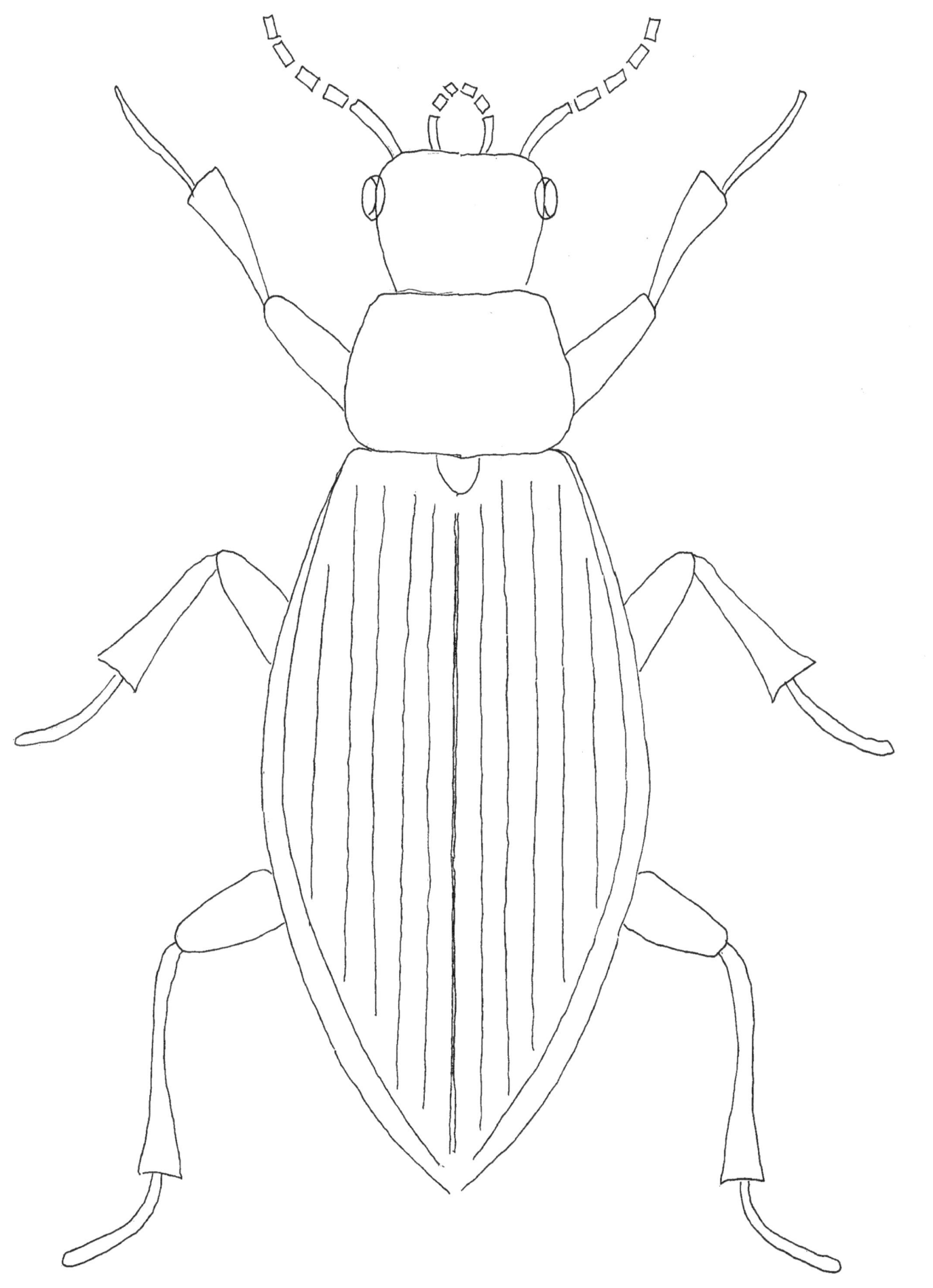

# The more light you allow within you, the brighter the world you live in will be.

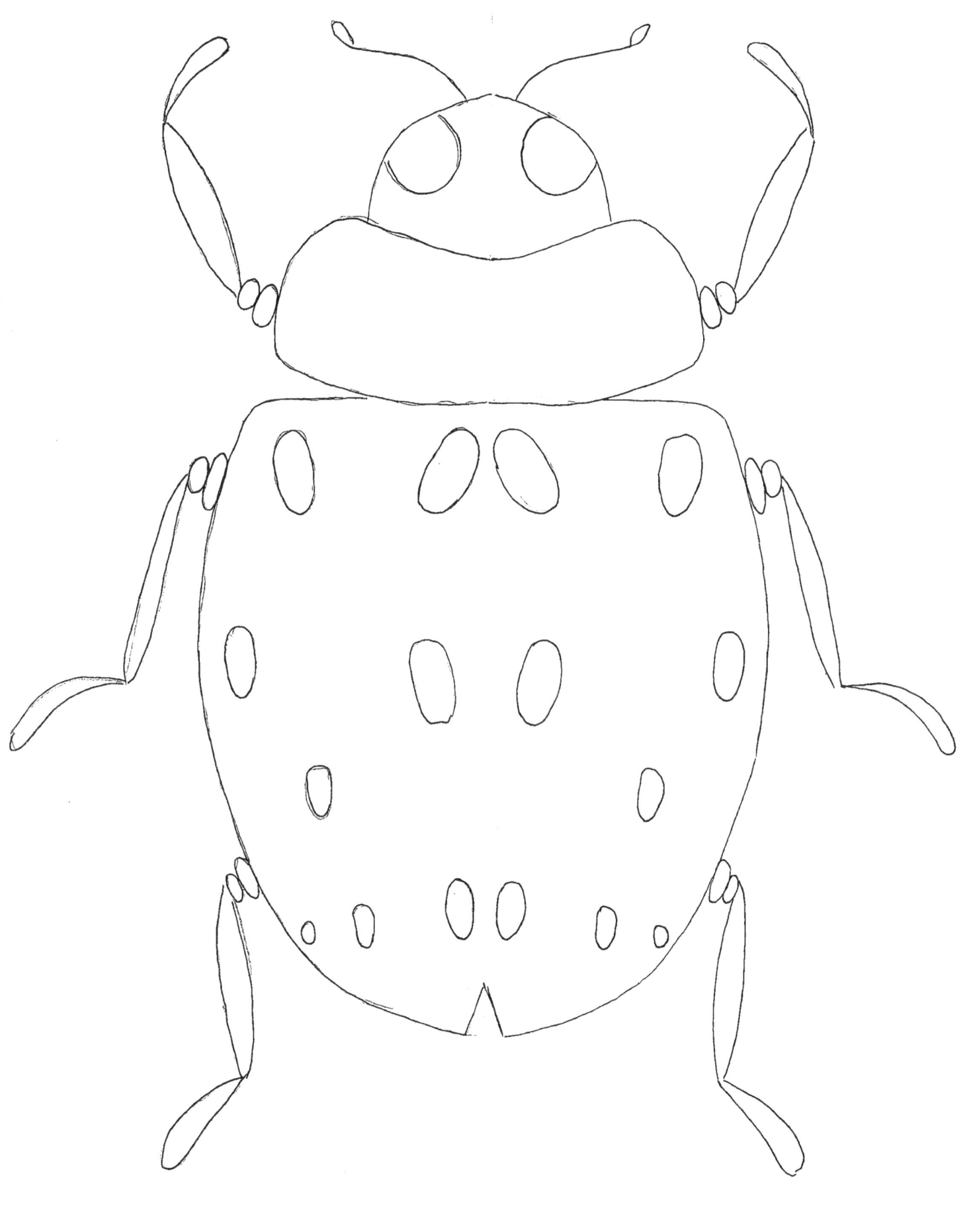

Journals are excellent ways to work through the "hard stuff" like, venting
your troubles, emotional distresses.

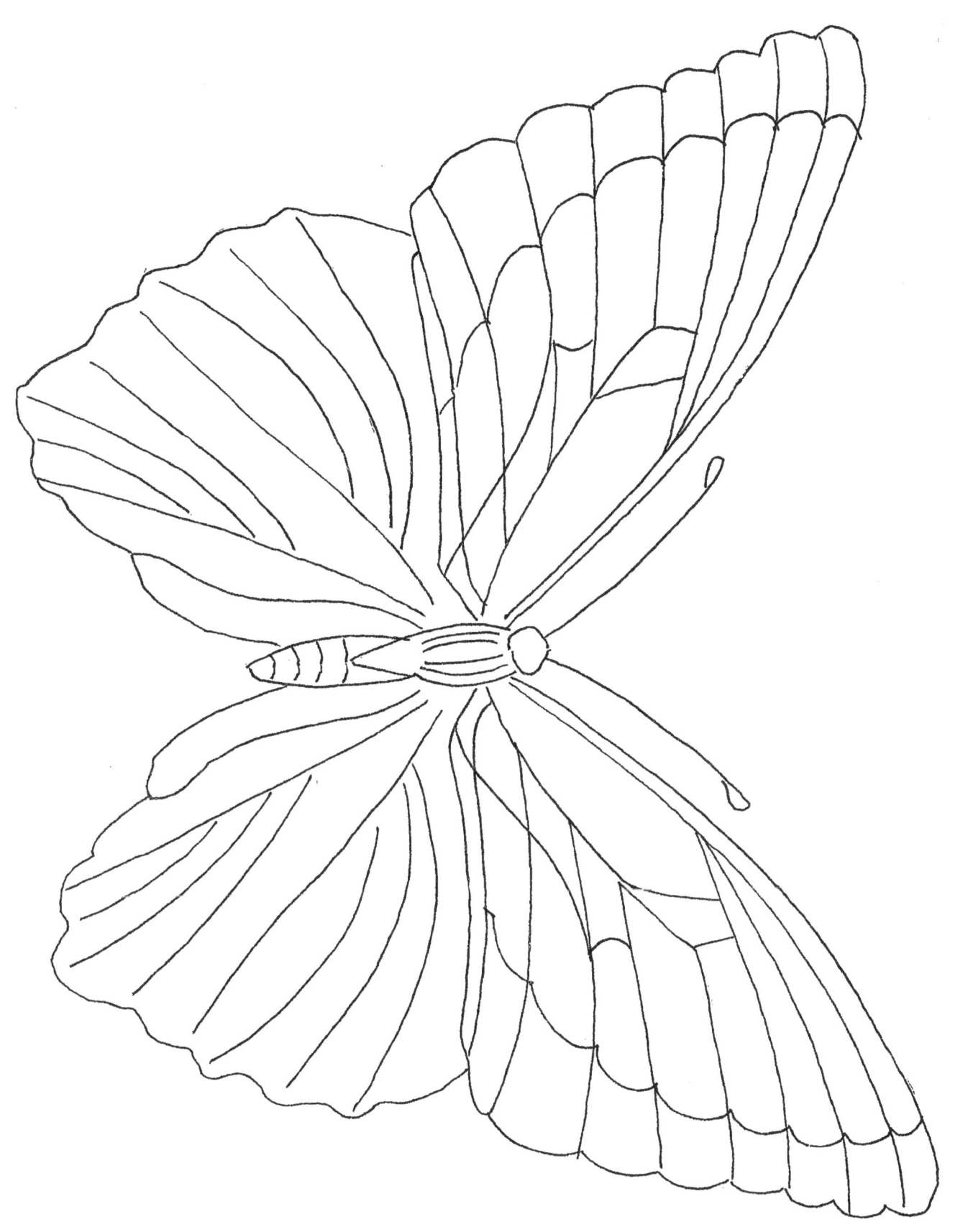

# Keeping a journal naturally reminds us to articulate next steps.

_____
_____
_____
_____
_____
_____
_____
_____
_____
_____
_____
_____
_____
_____
_____
_____
_____
_____
_____
_____
_____
_____
_____
_____
_____
_____
_____
_____
_____
_____

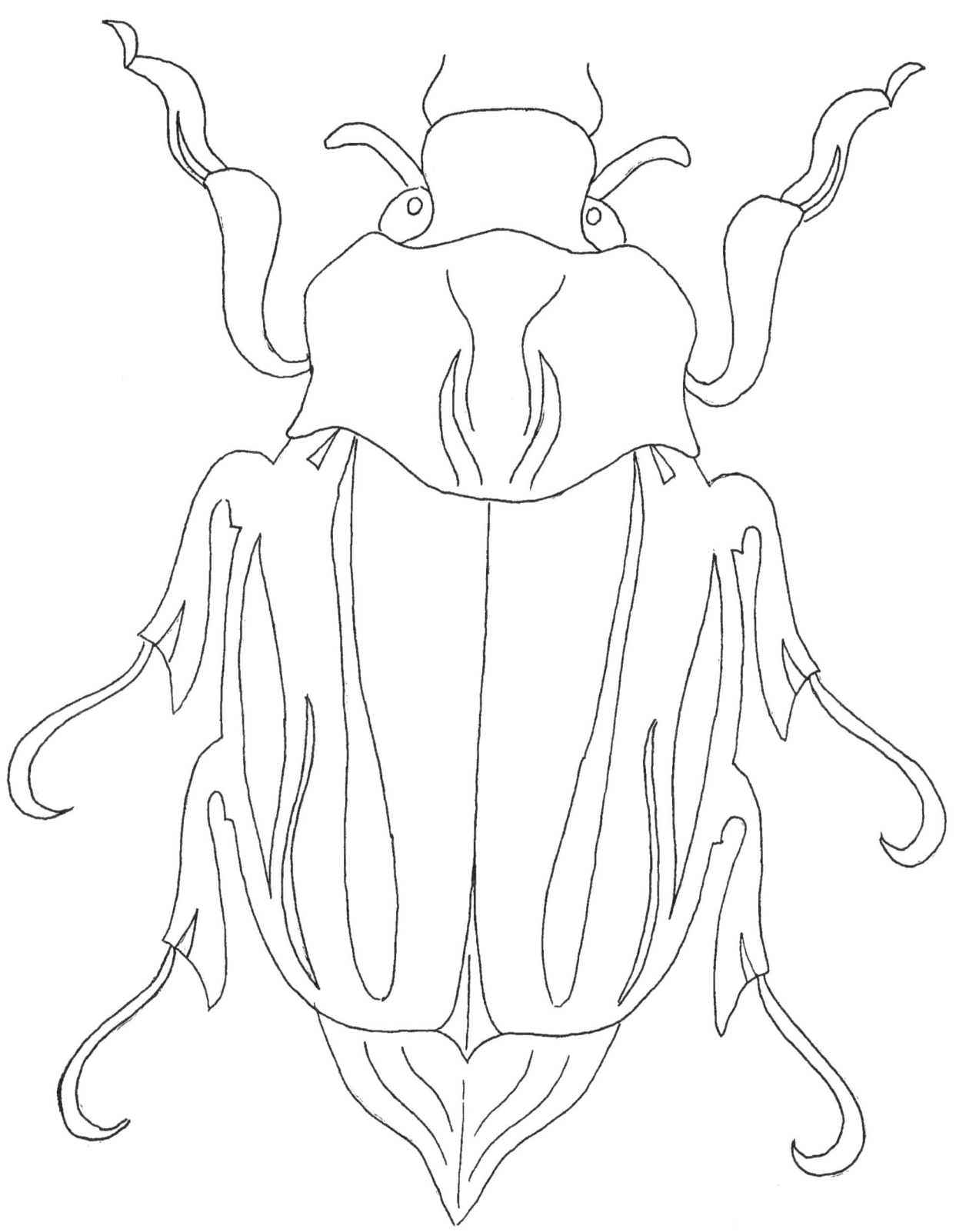

Keeping a journal helps us think through the why's and how's of situations.

_____

_____

_____

_____

_____

_____

_____

_____

_____

_____

_____

_____

_____

_____

_____

_____

_____

_____

_____

_____

_____

_____

_____

_____

_____

_____

_____

_____

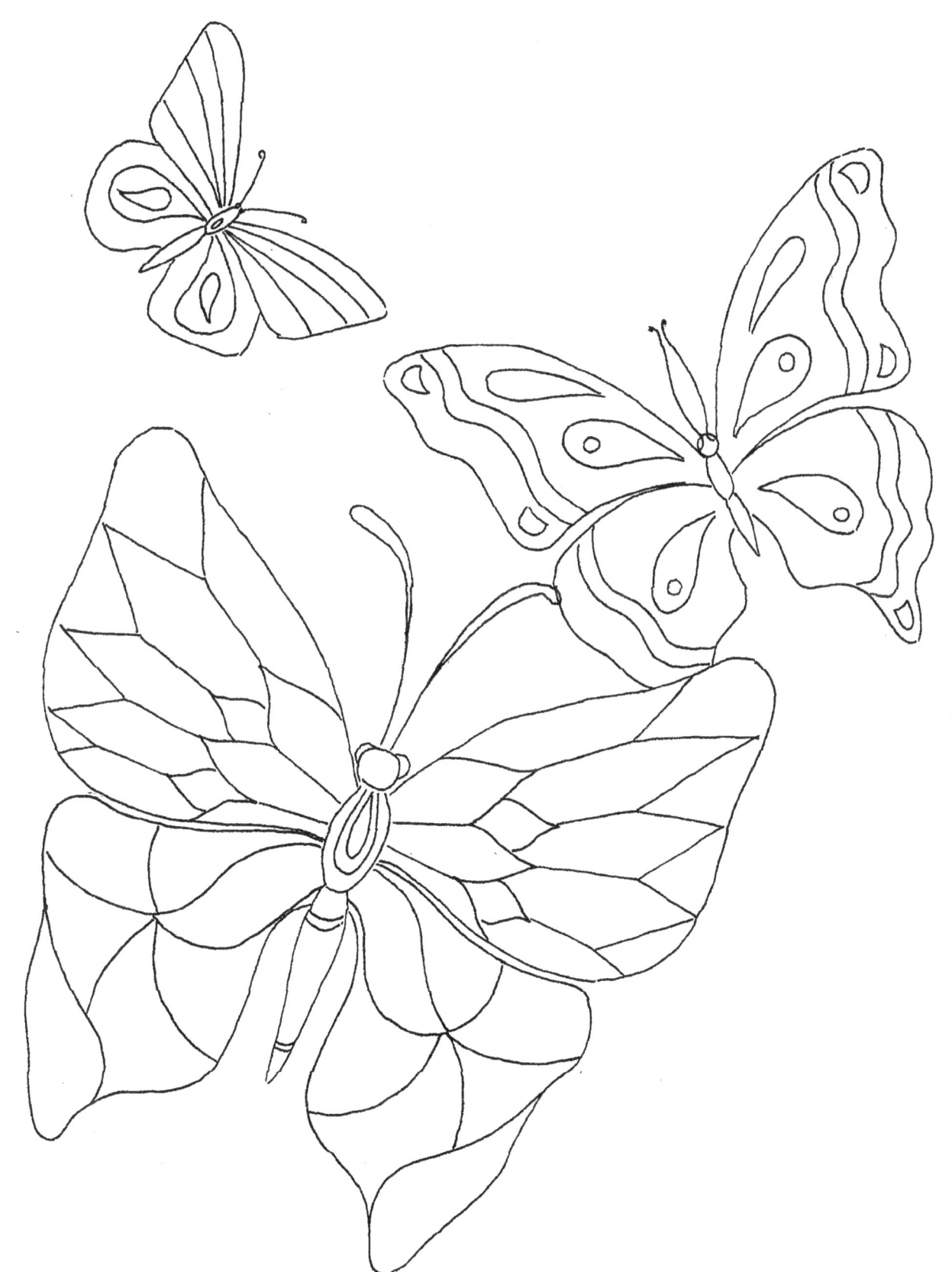

A journal serves as a permanent record of your progress.

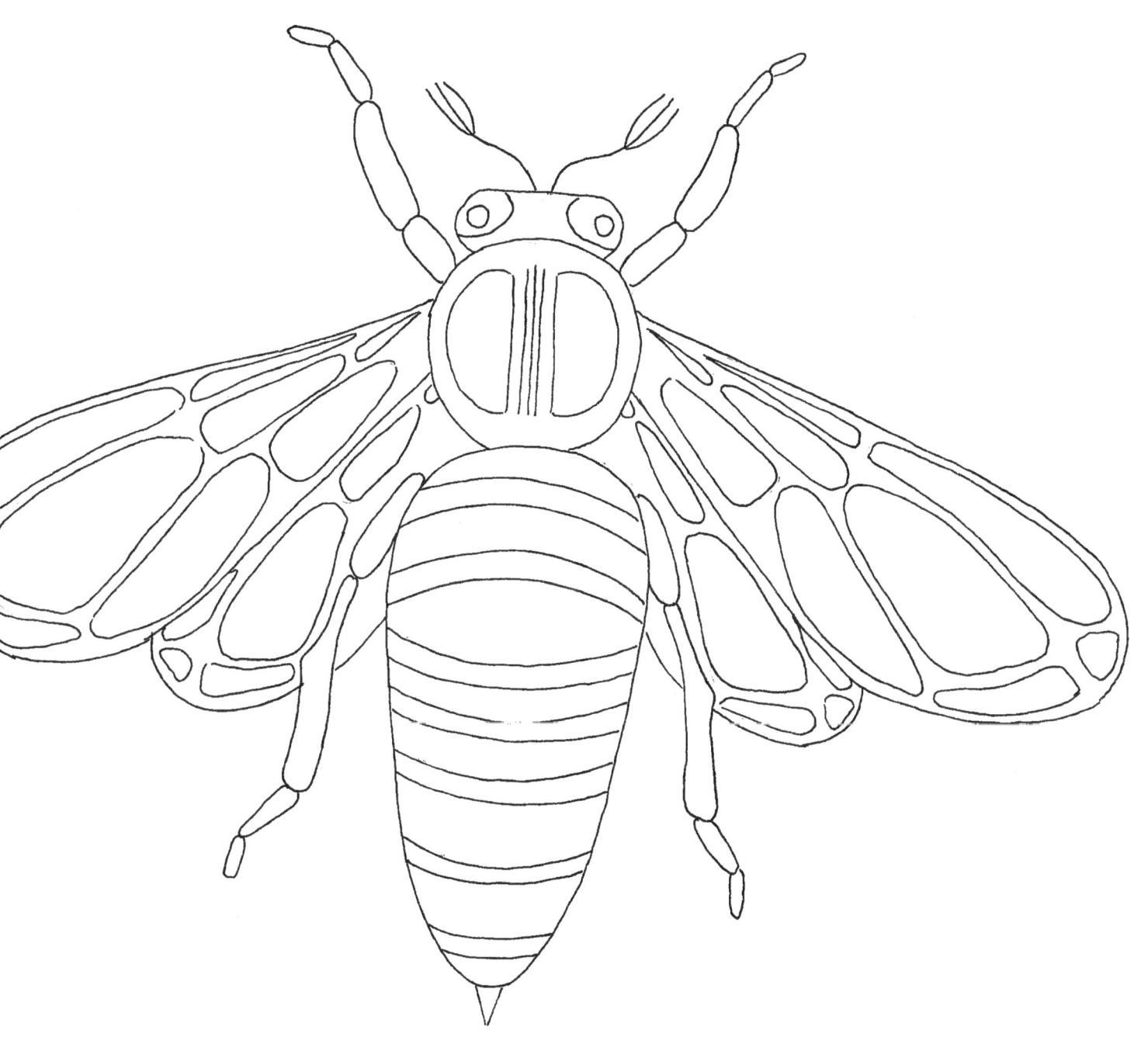

# Journaling your goals provide the opportunity to articulate them clearly and make their achievement appear closer.

_____
_____
_____
_____
_____
_____
_____
_____
_____
_____
_____
_____
_____
_____
_____
_____
_____
_____
_____
_____
_____
_____
_____
_____
_____
_____
_____
_____
_____
_____
_____
_____
_____
_____

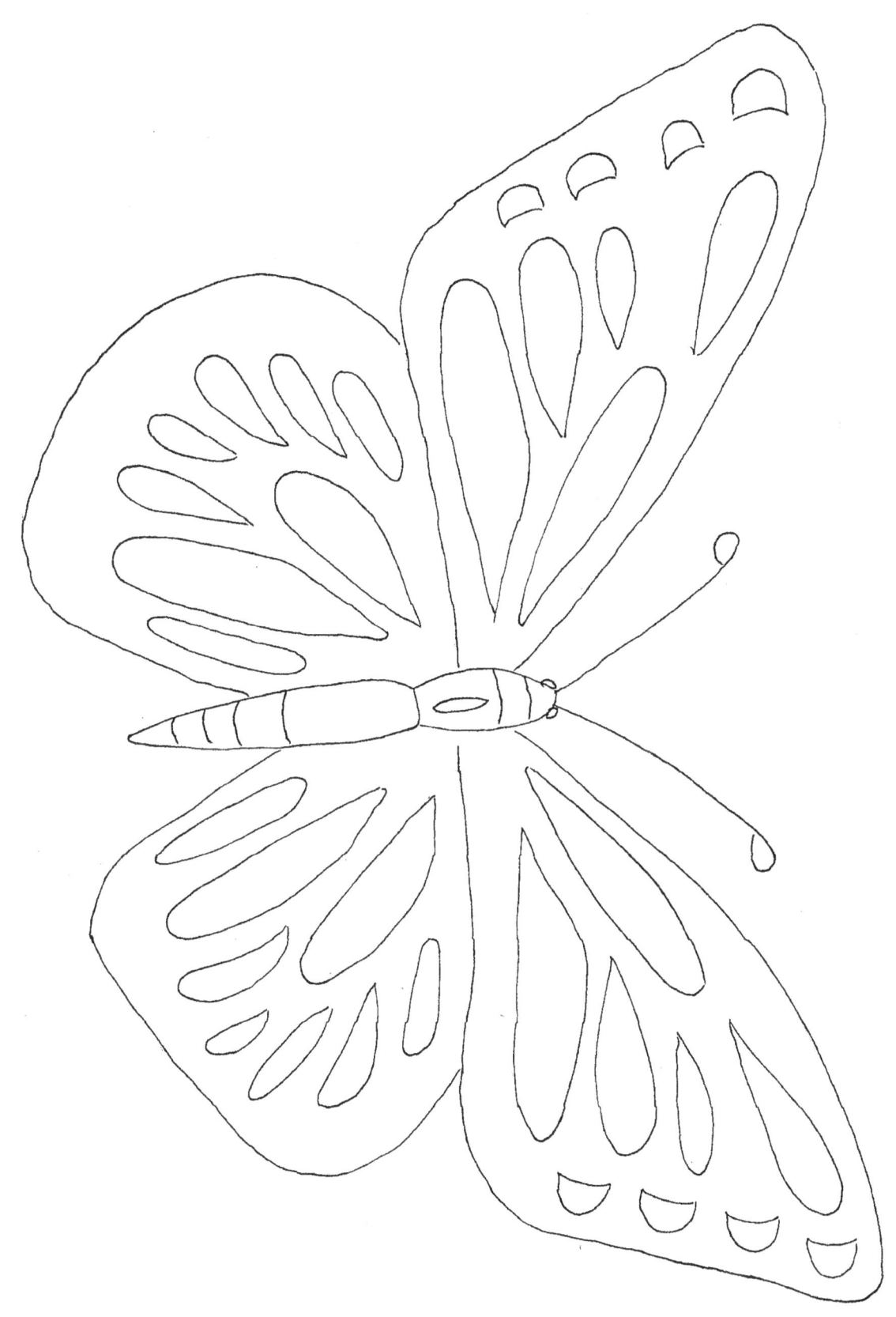

A journal give you permission to write yourself into history.

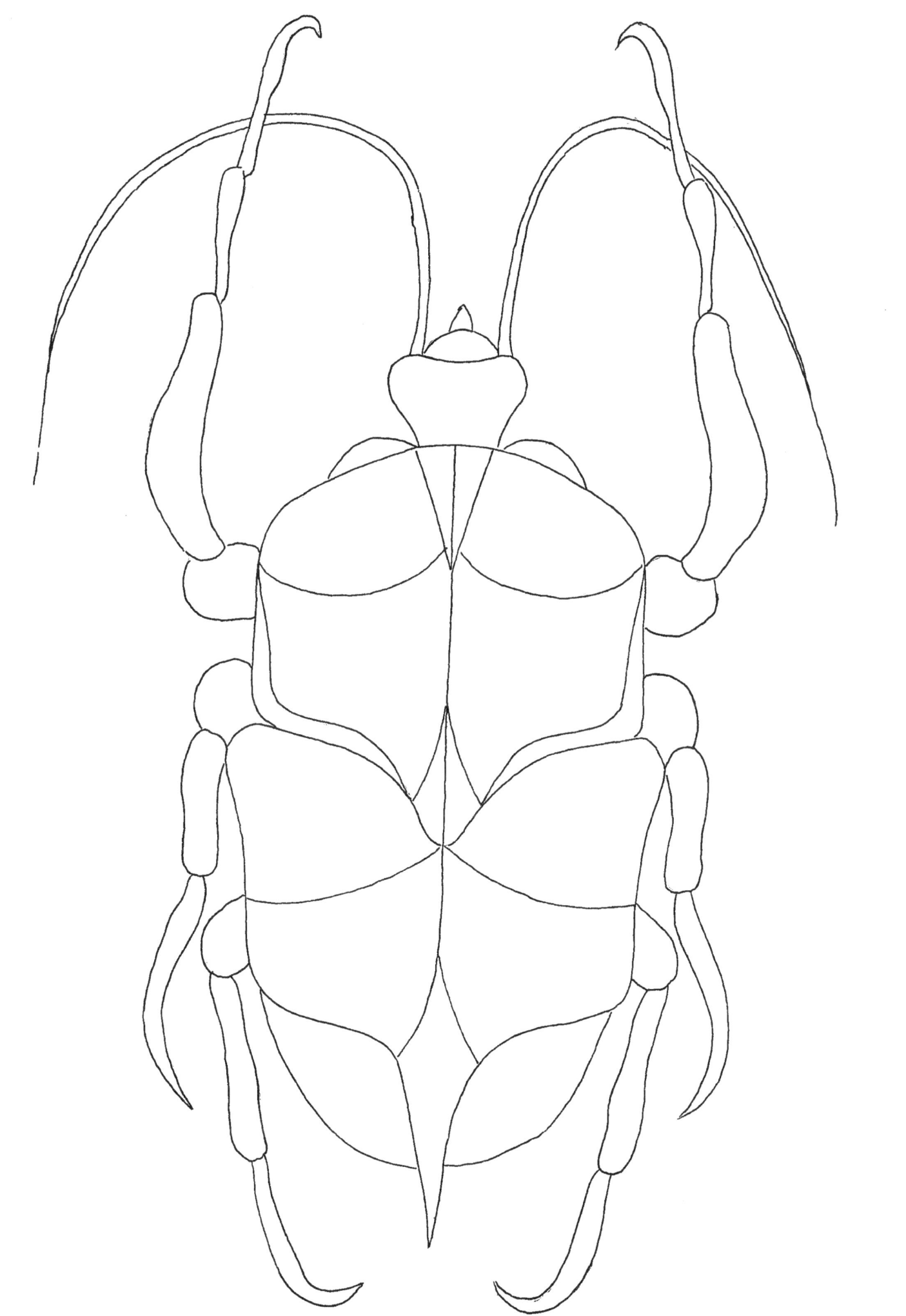

# Keeping a food journal is a great way to stay focused and pay closer attention to what you eat.

_____
_____
_____
_____
_____
_____
_____
_____
_____
_____
_____
_____
_____
_____
_____
_____
_____
_____
_____
_____
_____
_____
_____
_____
_____
_____
_____
_____
_____
_____
_____
_____
_____

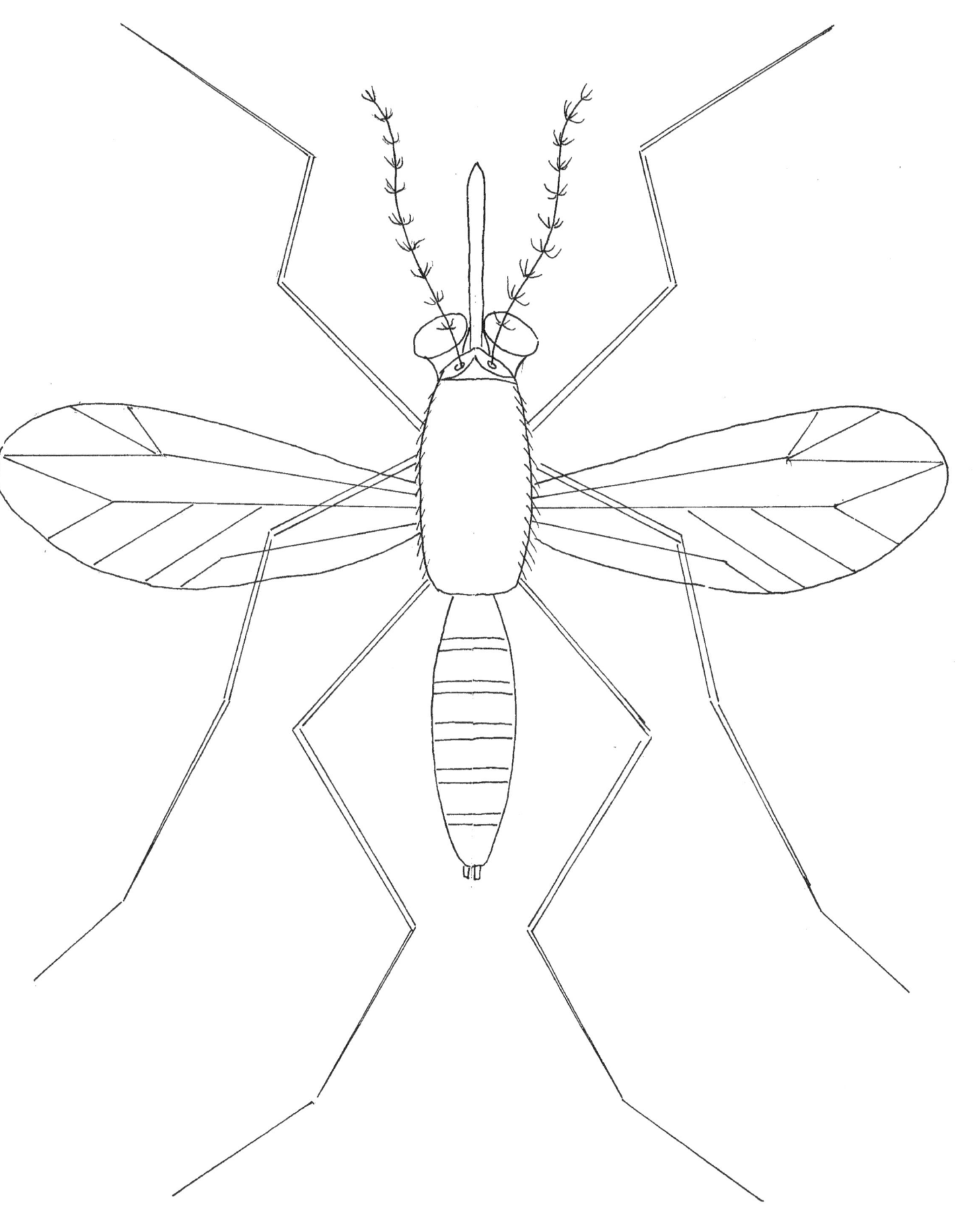

We are drawn to making our mark, leaving a record to show we were here, and a journal is a great place to do it.

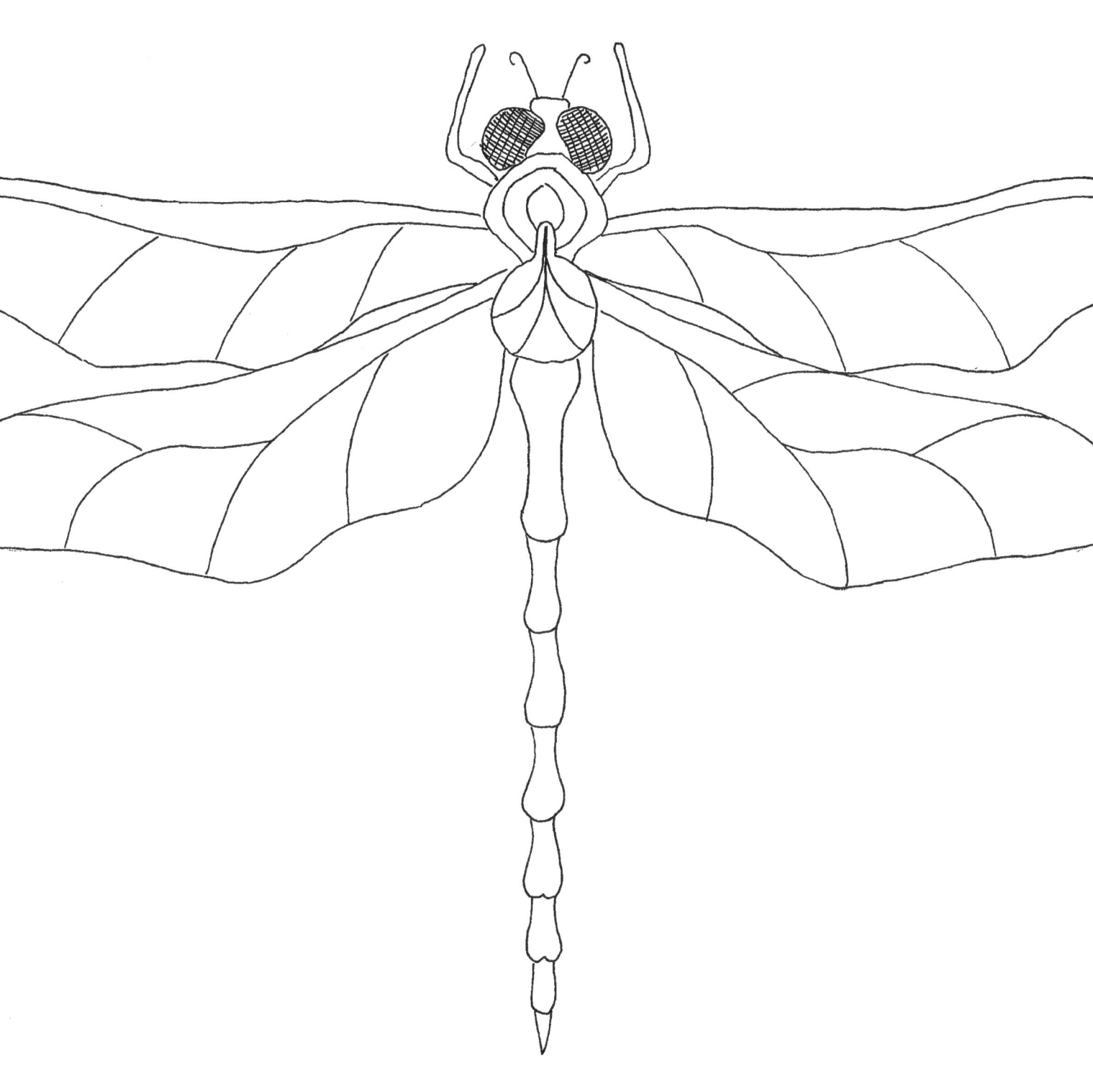

# Journaling has been specifically effective in people with severe illnesses, like cancer.

www.ingramcontent.com/pod-product-compliance
Lightning Source LLC
Chambersburg PA
CBHW080643190526
45169CB00009B/3480